# Hell

# Hell

Franklin Battle, Sr.

2007

# Hell

# TABLE OF CONTENTS

## SPECIAL THANKS

To my PK's, Franklin D. Battle Jr., Crystal G. Battle, and Lisa A. Battle, who have sacrificed so much by being PK's and encouraged me during ministry, my books, and projects.

To BriGette McCoy, Angela Gilliam, and Kanisa M. Reeves for their input, typing compiling, and proofing work and Lisa A. Battle for cover art work.

To Jesus Christ Ministries International Partners, Upper Room Church Family, and Project Real Life Youth Occupational Training Corp Inc. staff, thank you for your love and support during the inception and completion of this next level of ministry.

This book was a gift
From Corey Stephens @
BoA on 5/16/11

↳ Thanks Buddy

## APPRECIATION

### TO GOD

Who told me to write this book.

### TO MADELYN

My loving wife, who has supported and encouraged me in my work for the Lord and this book project. Her prayers and support mean so very much for all my book projects and ministry.

# INTRODUCTION

The Bible says that hell is a real place, and it also says that many people will spend eternity in that horrible place. God gives a lot of information about hell in the Bible, because His heart is to keep people from going there.

The average person has never taken the time to examine the biblical information about hell. One reason is that the verses about hell are distributed throughout the Bible. That can make it time-consuming to find them all. Therefore, my purpose here is to take those biblical facts and present them in an easy to read and easy to understand way.

It is my sincere hope that the people who read this book will realize that God's will is for everyone to avoid hell. God tells us that if we put our faith in the Lord Jesus Christ, we will go to a far better place called heaven where love, peace, and joy will last forever.

I always say that those who are on their way to hell have a math problem. They cannot calculate how long eternity will last. Eternity is FOREVER. If you lived to the age of one thousand, that would only be like one drop of water in the glass of eternity.

If you are not saved, I want to emphasize to you that the Lord Jesus is calling you to become a part of His precious family. So please accept this invitation by turning to the back of the book and praying the salvation prayer. This may be your last chance.

## WHAT IS HELL LIKE?

In this chapter, you will be given a glimpse of hell.

## OUTER DARKNESS

**Hell is described as *Outer Darkness.***

Imagine a house with many rooms in it, and all the lights are turned on at the same time. Each light is of the highest brightness you could possibly have. Now imagine the complete opposite as you step outside of the house. There are no streetlights, no moon, no stars, and no cars with headlights. It is like experiencing the darkest midnight. This is the picture that Jesus is painting when He says "outer darkness," is a place without God the Father or Himself.

We read about "outer darkness" three times in Matthew's gospel. The first reference is Matthew 8:12, the second is Matthew 22:13, and the third time is Matthew 25:30. Only one verse will be highlighted here. You will see all of these verses in context in the appendix.

*Matthew 25:30*
*25 "And cast the unprofitable servant into the outer darkness. There will be weeping and gnashing of teeth."*

## COMPARING DARKNESS WITH LIGHT

Contrast this picture of the depressing darkness of hell to the glorious light of the New Jerusalem in the following verses:

*Revelation 21:9-11, 22-23*
*9 Then one of the seven angels who had the seven bowls filled with the seven last plagues came to me and talked with me, saying, "Come, I will show you the bride, the Lamb's wife."*
*10 And he carried me away in the Spirit to a great and high mountain, and showed me the great city, the holy Jerusalem, descending out of heaven from God,*
*11 having the glory of God. Her light was like a most precious stone, like a jasper stone, clear as crystal.*
*22 But I saw no temple in it, for the Lord God Almighty and the Lamb are its temple.*
*23 The city had no need of the sun or of the moon to shine in it, for the glory of God illuminated it. The Lamb is its light.*

Now that we have established how dark it is, let's observe some of the other characteristics of hell.

## FIRE

Fire is the best-known image associated with hell. The fire of hell is eternal and will never go out. It will burn its victims constantly with heat so hot that it burns the soul *and* spirit.

*Luke 16:24*
*24 "Then he cried and said, 'Father Abraham, have mercy on me, and send Lazarus that he may dip the tip of his finger in water and cool my tongue; for I am tormented in this flame.'"*

## EVERLASTING FIRE

*Matthew 25:41*

41 "Then He will also say to those on the left hand, 'Depart from Me, you cursed, into the everlasting fire prepared for the devil and his angels:'"

## FURNACE OF FIRE

*Matthew 13:36-42, 47-50*

36 Then Jesus sent the multitude away and went into the house. And His disciples came to Him, saying, "Explain to us the parable of the tares of the field."

37 He answered and said to them: "He who sows the good seed is the Son of Man.

38 The field is the world, the good seeds are the sons of the kingdom, but the tares are the sons of the wicked one.

39 The enemy who sowed them is the devil, the harvest is the end of the age, and the reapers are the angels.

40 Therefore as the tares are gathered and burned in the fire, so it will be at the end of this age.

41 The Son of Man will send out His angels, and they will gather out of His kingdom all things that offend, and those who practice lawlessness,

42 and will cast them into the furnace of fire. There will be wailing and gnashing of teeth."

47 "Again, the kingdom of heaven is like a dragnet that was cast into the sea and gathered some of every kind,

48 which, when it was full, they drew to shore; and they sat down and gathered the good into vessels, but threw the bad away.

49 So it will be at the end of the age. The angels will come forth, separate the wicked from among the just,

50 and cast them into the furnace of fire. There will be wailing (cry bitterly*) and gnashing of teeth."

*Added

## WORMS

In light of the biblical verses about hell, it seems that worms will probably be a part of the tormenting process. The scriptures are not very clear on them or their role in hell. They have to be spiritual beings, because we are talking about a spiritual place that was made for Satan and his angels.

*Mark 9:44-48*
*44 "where 'Their worm does not die, And the fire is not quenched.'*
*45 And if your foot causes you to sin, cut it off. It is better for you to enter life lame, rather than having two feet, to be cast into hell, into the fire that shall never be quenched -*
*46 where 'Their worm does not die, And the fire is not quenched.'*
*47 And if your eye causes you to sin, pluck it out. It is better for you to enter the kingdom of God with one eye, rather than having two eyes, to be cast into hell fire—*
*48 where 'Their worm does not die, And the fire is not quenched.'"*

## WEEPING AND GNASHING OF TEETH

Weeping and gnashing of teeth brings to mind the idea of crying intensely and grinding the teeth back and forth. It will be a state of severe pain and agony for all eternity.

*Matthew 22:13, 25:30*
*13 "Then the king said to the servants, 'Bind him hand and foot, take him away, and cast him into outer darkness; there will be weeping and gnashing of teeth.'"*
*30 "And cast the unprofitable servant into the outer darkness. There will be weeping and gnashing of teeth."*

## A PIT

The Bible sometimes describes hell as a pit. Dark and dank, those in a pit are trapped. They are helpless to be released from their deep prison.

*Psalm 30:3*
*3 O Lord, You brought my soul up from the grave; You have kept me alive, that I should not go down to the pit.*

*Revelation 9:1-2*
*1 Then the fifth angel sounded: And I saw a star fallen from heaven to the earth. To him was given the key to the bottomless pit.*
*2 And he opened the bottomless pit, and smoke arose out of the pit like the smoke of a great furnace. So the sun and the air were darkened because of the smoke of the pit.*

*Revelation 20: 1-3*
*1 Then I saw an angel coming down from heaven, having the key to the bottomless pit and a great chain in his hand.*
*2 He laid hold of the dragon, that serpent of old, who is the Devil and Satan, and bound him for a thousand years;*
*3 and he cast him into the bottomless pit, and shut him up, and set a seal on him, so that he should deceive the nations no more till the thousand years were finished. But after these things he must be released for a little while.*

## EVERLASTING PUNISHMENT

Hell is always pictured as punishment.

*Matthew 25:46*
*46 "And these will go away into everlasting punishment, but the righteous into eternal life."*

## EVERLASTING DESTRUCTION

*2 Thessalonians 1:7-10*
*7 and to give you who are troubled rest with us when the Lord Jesus is revealed from heaven with His mighty angels,*
*8 in flaming fire taking vengeance on those who do not know God, and on those who do not obey the gospel of our Lord Jesus Christ.*
*9 These shall be punished with everlasting destruction from the presence of the Lord and from the glory of His power,*
*10 when He comes, in that Day, to be glorified in His saints and to be admired among all those who believe, because our testimony among you was believed.*

## TORMENTING OR TORTURE

The word "torture" can be defined as THE ACT OF IN-FLICTING EXCRUCIATING PAIN, ESPECIALLY AS A MEANS OF PUNISHMENT OR COERCION.

Torture gives the victim extreme physical, mental, or spiritual pain, and anguish.

Revelations 14:11 says that those people who worship the beast and his image and receive the mark of his name will experience torment.

*Revelations 14:11*
*11 "And the smoke of their torment ascends forever and ever; and they have no rest day or night, who worship the beast and his image, and whoever receives the mark of his name."*

In Mark 5:7, we read about how demons feel about the prospect of being tormented in hell.

*Mark 5:7*
*7 And he cried out {the demon} with a loud voice and said, "What have I to do with You, Jesus, Son of the Most High God? I implore You by God that You do not torment me."*

In the previous verse, the demons are begging Jesus not to torment them. Now if the demons can't stand the pain of being tormented, what do you think will be the condition of human souls that will undergo an eternity of this treatment?

## CONCLUDING WORDS

In reading the above scriptures, we find hell to be dark, dismal, gloomy, a place of sorrow, and a place of suffering. Pain is ever present. Those in hell feel the tormenting sensation of burning and the ache of loneliness. Jesus teaches that those in hell have a clear memory of their life on earth. The clarity of a person's memories on earth increases the suffering as the person recalls that he or she had the opportunity to be in heaven.

## THE NAMES OF HELL

**Hell has many names.**

Hell by any other name is still *torment.* No matter what name is used for hell, the picture represented is one that embodies painful, tormenting horror for its inhabitants.

The word "hell" is an English word used to describe the place of torment that will be the eternal home of Satan, the demons (also known as fallen angels), and people who have not placed their trust in Jesus as Lord and Savior.

There are several other names for the place we call hell.

## SHEOL

This was the Old Testament Hebrew word for the abode of the dead.

*Psalms 16:10*
*10 For You will not leave my soul in Sheol, Nor will You allow Your Holy One to see corruption.*

## HADES

The Greek word for hell is hades.

*Revelation 20:14*
*14 Then Death and Hades were cast into the lake of fire. This is the second death.*

## FURNACE OF FIRE

*Matthew 13:42*
*42 "and will cast them into the furnace of fire. There will be wailing and gnashing of teeth."*

## GEHENNA

This is another Greek word for hell that occurs 12 times in the New Testament. Interestingly 11 of the 12 times, it was Jesus who used the word. Gehenna means everlasting destruction. The people living in the time of Jesus knew Gehenna as a garbage dump that had once been a place of human sacrifice. It is believed by many historians that the dump burned continually day and night.

In the following verse, the word translated "hell' is the Greek word "Gehenna."

*Matthew 23:15*
*15 "Woe to you, scribes and Pharisees, hypocrites! For you travel land and sea to win one proselyte, and when he is won, you make him twice as much a son of hell as yourselves."*

## HELL'S BIG SISTER—THE LAKE OF FIRE

This is a place bigger than hell, and will contain more people than the original hell. Hell will be cast into it. The torment will be greater in this place.

*Revelations 19:20*
*20 Then the beast was captured, and with him the false prophet who worked signs in his presence, by which he deceived those who received the mark of the beast and those who worshiped his image. These two were cast alive into the lake of fire burning with brimstone.*

*Revelations 20:10, 14-15*
*10 The devil, who deceived them, was cast into the lake of fire and brimstone where the beast and the false prophet are. And they will be tormented day and night forever and ever.*
*14 Then Death and Hades (or Hell) were cast into the lake of fire. This is the second death.*
*15 And anyone not found written in the Book of Life was cast into the lake of fire.*

*Revelations 21:8*
*8 But the cowardly, unbelieving, abominable, murderers, sexually immoral, sorcerers, idolaters, and all liars shall have their part in the lake which burns with fire and brimstone, which is the second death."*

## TARTAROS

In the Greek culture, tartaros was the lowest level in hades. This word is used only once in the Bible in 2 Peter 2:4. English Bible translators usually put the word "hell" in its place. We see this in the following verse.

*2 Peter 2:4*
*4 For if God did not spare the angels who sinned, but cast them down to hell and delivered them into chains of darkness, to be reserved for judgment;*

## LOWEST HELL

*Deuteronomy 32:22*
22 "For a fire is kindled in My anger, And shall burn to the lowest hell;
It shall consume the earth with her increase, And set on fire the founda-
tions of the mountains."

## WHY WAS HELL MADE?

The simple answer is that hell was made for Satan and his demonic angels.

## AN EVERLASTING FIRE PREPARED FOR SATAN AND HIS ANGELS

The final destination for Satan and all his demonic angels is hell. To be specific, it is the Lake of Fire.

*Matthew 25:41*
*41 "Then He will also say to those on the left hand, 'Depart from Me, you cursed, into the everlasting fire prepared for the devil and his angels:'"*

## SATAN'S EARLY HISTORY

How did Satan get on the *Road to Hell?*
Satan was created as a cherub of God. In the next verses, we hear God describing Lucifer's rebellious rages against God. (Satan was created Lucifer.)

*Isaiah 14:9-17*
*9 "Hell from beneath is excited about you, To meet you at your coming; It stirs up the dead for you, All the chief ones of the earth; It has raised up from their thrones All the kings of the nations.*
*10 They all shall speak and say to you: 'Have you also become as weak as we? Have you become like us?*

*11 Your pomp is brought down to Sheol, And the sound of your stringed instruments; The maggot is spread under you, And worms cover you."'*

*12 "How you are fallen from heaven, O Lucifer, son of the morning! How you are cut down to the ground, You who weakened the nations!*

*13 For you have said in your heart: 'I will ascend into heaven. I will exalt my throne above the stars of God; I will also sit on the mount of the congregation On the farthest sides of the north;*

*14 I will ascend above the heights of the clouds, I will be like the Most High.'*

*15 Yet you shall be brought down to Sheol, To the lowest depths of the Pit."*

*16 "Those who see you will gaze at you, And consider you, saying: 'Is this the man who made the earth tremble, Who shook kingdoms,*

*17 Who made the world as a wilderness And destroyed its cities, Who did not open the house of his prisoners?'"'*

Next, we see verses about Satan in the early part of his history on earth. We find that he was created as the anointed cherub who covers.

*Ezekiel 28:13-14*

*13 "You were in Eden, the garden of God; Every precious stone was your covering: The sardius, topaz, and diamond, Beryl, onyx, and jasper, Sapphire, turquoise, and emerald with gold. The workmanship of your timbrels and pipes Was prepared for you on the day you were created."*

*14 "You were the anointed cherub who covers; I established you; You were on the holy mountain of God; You walked back and forth in the midst of fiery stones."*

## FALLEN ANGELS

When Lucifer sinned, he was able to convince a large number of angels to follow him instead of God. Many scholars believe that one third of the angels united with Lucifer. They usually point to the following scripture as the origin of the one-third number.

(Fallen angels are demons.)

*Revelation 12:4a*
*4 His tail drew a third of the stars of heaven and threw them to the earth.*

*2 Peter 2:4*
*4 For if God did not spare the angels who sinned, but cast them down to hell and delivered them into chains of darkness, to be reserved for judgment;*

## ONE THOUSAND YEARS

Before the end comes for Satan, there will be a time when Satan is bound and cast into a bottomless pit for one thousand years.

*Revelation 20:1-15*
*1 Then I saw an angel coming down from heaven, having the key to the bottomless pit and a great chain in his hand.*
*2 He laid hold of the dragon, that serpent of old, who is the Devil and Satan, and bound him for a thousand years;*
*3 and he cast him into the bottomless pit, and shut him up, and set a seal on him, so that he should deceive the nations no more till the thousand years were finished. But after these things he must be released for a little while.*
*4 And I saw thrones, and they sat on them, and judgment was committed to them. Then I saw the souls of those who had been beheaded for their witness to Jesus and for the word of God, who had not worshiped the beast or his image, and had not received his mark on their foreheads or on their hands. And they lived and reigned with Christ for a thousand years.*

*5 But the rest of the dead did not live again until the thousand years were finished. This is the first resurrection.*

*6 Blessed and holy is he who has part in the first resurrection. Over such the second death has no power, but they shall be priests of God and of Christ, and shall reign with Him a thousand years.*

*7 Now when the thousand years have expired, Satan will be released from his prison*

*8 and will go out to deceive the nations which are in the four corners of the earth, Gog and Magog, to gather them together to battle, whose number is as the sand of the sea.*

*9 They went up on the breadth of the earth and surrounded the camp of the saints and the beloved city. And fire came down from God out of heaven and devoured them.*

*10 The devil, who deceived them, was cast into the lake of fire and brimstone where the beast and the false prophet are. And they will be tormented day and night forever and ever.*

*11 Then I saw a great white throne and Him who sat on it, from whose face the earth and the heaven fled away. And there was found no place for them.*

*12 And I saw the dead, small and great, standing before God, and books were opened. And another book was opened, which is the Book of Life. And the dead were judged according to their works, by the things which were written in the books.*

*13 The sea gave up the dead who were in it, and Death and Hades delivered up the dead who were in them. And they were judged, each one according to his works.*

*14 Then Death and Hades were cast into the lake of fire. This is the second death.*

*15 And anyone not found written in the Book of Life was cast into the lake of fire.*

## UNBELIEVERS

Even though hell was made for the devil and his demons, all people who do not put their trust in Jesus will be cast into hell also.

When a person receives salvation, that person's name is written in the Book of Life. The next verses explain that if someone's name is not in the Book of Life, that person will be cast into the lake of fire.

*Revelation 20:10-15*
*10 The devil, who deceived them, was cast into the lake of fire and brimstone where the beast and the false prophet are. And they will be tormented day and night forever and ever.*
*11 Then I saw a great white throne and Him who sat on it, from whose face the earth and the heaven fled away. And there was found no place for them.*
*12 And I saw the dead, small and great, standing before God, and books were opened. And another book was opened, which is the Book of Life. And the dead were judged according to their works, by the things which were written in the books.*
*13 The sea gave up the dead who were in it, and Death and Hades delivered up the dead who were in them. And they were judged, each one according to his works.*
*14 Then Death and Hades were cast into the lake of fire. This is the second death.*
*15 And anyone not found written in the Book of Life was cast into the lake of fire.*

## THE RESIDENTS OF HELL

The Bible tells us who will be living in hell. This chapter will explain who the occupants of hell will be. Unless the people who are described in this section repent and ask Jesus to be their Lord and Savior, they will find themselves in hell after they take their last breath.

### PERDITION

The definition of the word "perdition" is the state of the damned. Those who are on their way to hell are the children of perdition.

*2 Thessalonians 2:1-12*
*1 Now, brethren, concerning the coming of our Lord Jesus Christ and our gathering together to Him, we ask you,*
*2 not to be soon shaken in mind or troubled, either by spirit or by word or by letter, as if from us, as though the day of Christ had come.*
*3 Let no one deceive you by any means; for that Day will not come unless the falling away comes first, and the man of sin is revealed, the son of perdition,*
*4 who opposes and exalts himself above all that is called God or that is worshiped, so that he sits as God in the temple of God, showing himself that he is God.*
*5 Do you not remember that when I was still with you I told you these things?*
*6 And now you know what is restraining, that he may be revealed in his own time.*

*7 For the mystery of lawlessness is already at work; only He who now restrains will do so until He is taken out of the way.*

*8 And then the lawless one will be revealed, whom the Lord will consume with the breath of His mouth and destroy with the brightness of His coming.*

*9 The coming of the lawless one is according to the working of Satan, with all power, signs, and lying wonders,*

*10 and with all unrighteous deception among those who perish, because they did not receive the love of the truth, that they might be saved.*

*11 And for this reason God will send them strong delusion, that they should believe the lie,*

*12 that they all may be condemned who did not believe the truth but had pleasure in unrighteousness.*

## CHAPTER DIVISIONS:

For the rest of this chapter, "The Residents of Hell" will be divided into four different lists.

The first list is for groups who are directly or indirectly referred to in the Bible. For the average Christian, the people in this group will be somewhat obvious residents of hell.

The second list is comprised of false religions that were in existence during the time of the Bible. These old religious systems are still drawing unsuspecting victims today.

The third list highlights false religions, movements, or political systems that were started after the Bible was written. Those in this list have direct ties to anti-God teachings.

The fourth list contains individuals whose sins are specifically spelled out as sins. The Bible tells us that these people are headed toward hell.

**The First List**
**Those who are directly or indirectly referred to in the Bible**

### ATHEISTS

Those who believe there is no God

*Psalm 53:1*
*1 The fool has said in his heart, "There is no God."*

### AGNOSTICS

Those who doubt the existence of God—also called unbelievers

*Revelation 21:8*
*8 "But the cowardly, unbelieving, abominable, murderers, sexually immoral, sorcerers, idolaters, and all liars shall have their part in the lake which burns with fire and brimstone, which is the second death."*

### ASTROLOGERS

Those who study the supposed influences of the stars and planets on human affairs

*Isaiah 47:12-14*
*12 "Stand now with your enchantments And the multitude of your sorceries, in which you have labored from your youth—Perhaps you will be able to profit, Perhaps you will prevail.*

*13 You are wearied in the multitude of your counsels; Let now the astrologers, the stargazers, And the monthly prognosticators Stand up and save you From what shall come upon you.*

*14 Behold, they shall be as stubble, The fires shall burn them; They shall not deliver themselves From the power of the flame; It shall not be a coal to be warmed by, Nor a fire to sit before!"*

## ANTICHRISTS

People who are against, or say they are a substitute for, Christ

*1 John 2:18*
*18 Little children, it is the last hour; and as you have heard that the Antichrist is coming, even now many antichrists have come, by which we know that it is the last hour.*

*I John 2:22*
*22 Who is a liar but he who denies that Jesus is the Christ? He is antichrist who denies the Father and the Son.*

## THE ANTICHRIST

A man who will live and rule during the last days before Christ returns

*1 John 2:18*
*18 Little children, it is the last hour; and as you have heard that the Antichrist is coming, even now many antichrists have come, by which we know that it is the last hour.*

## FALSE PROPHETS

Those who falsely claim inspiration of God; they give false words and say they are from God

*Matthew 7:15*
*15 "Beware of false prophets, who come to you in sheep's clothing, but inwardly they are ravenous wolves."*

## THE FALSE PROPHET

The chief religious figure in the world during the tribulation

*Revelation 19:20*
*20 Then the beast was captured, and with him the false prophet who worked signs in his presence, by which he deceived those who received the mark of the beast and those who worshiped his image. These two were cast alive into the lake of fire burning with brimstone.*

*Revelation 20:10*
*10 The devil, who deceived them, was cast into the lake of fire and brimstone where the beast and the false prophet are. And they will be tormented day and night forever and ever.*

## FALSE TEACHERS

Those who instruct contrary to God's will

*2 Peter 2:1-2*
*1 But there were also false prophets among the people, even as there will be false teachers among you, who will secretly bring in destructive heresies, even denying the Lord who bought them, and bring on themselves swift destruction.*
*2 And many will follow their destructive ways, because of whom the way of truth will be blasphemed.*

## FORTUNE-TELLERS

Those who profess to predict the future using methods that God forbids

*Leviticus 19:26 NLT*
*26 "Do not eat meat that has not been drained of its blood. Do not practice fortune-telling or witchcraft."*

*Acts 16:16-19*
*16 Now it happened, as we went to prayer, that a certain slave girl possessed with a spirit of divination met us, who brought her masters much profit by fortune-telling.*
*17 This girl followed Paul and us, and cried out, saying, "These men are the servants of the Most High God, who proclaim to us the way of salvation."*
*18 And this she did for many days. But Paul, greatly annoyed, turned and said to the spirit, "I command you in the name of Jesus Christ to come out of her." And he came out that very hour.*
*19 But when her masters saw that their hope of profit was gone, they seized Paul and Silas and dragged them into the marketplace to the authorities.*

## MAGICIANS

Those who practice the art of doing superhuman things by supernatural means; they also use illusions or sleight of hand; magic is a doorway to sorcery

*Exodus 7:10-12*
*10 So Moses and Aaron went in to Pharaoh and they did so, just as the Lord commanded. And Aaron cast down his rod before Pharaoh and before his servants, and it became a serpent.*

*11 But Pharaoh also called the wise men and the sorcerers; so the magicians of Egypt, they also did in like manner with their enchantments.*
*12 For every man threw down his rod, and they became serpents. But Aaron's rod swallowed up their rods.*

## MEDIUMS

Those through whom supposed messages from the world of spirits are received and sent

*2 Kings 21:6*
*6 Also he {Manasseh} made his son pass through the fire, practiced soothsaying, used witchcraft, and consulted spiritists and mediums. He did much evil in the sight of the Lord, to provoke Him {God} to anger.*

## PALM READERS

Those who look at the lines in one's hands and attempt to give information about the person from the lines

*Acts 19:19-20 KJV*
*19 Many of them also which used curious arts brought their books together, and burned them before all men: and they counted the price of them, and found it fifty thousand pieces of silver.*
*20 So mightily grew the word of God and prevailed.*

## PSYCHICS

Those who are especially sensitive to psychic influences or forces; a psychic is a medium

*Deuteronomy 18:10b-12a NLT*
*10 "And do not let your people practice fortune-telling, or use sorcery, or interpret omens, or engage in witchcraft,*

*11 or cast spells, or function as mediums or psychics, or call forth the spirits of the dead.*
*12 Anyone who does these things is detestable to the Lord."*

## SORCERERS

People who use power gained from evil spirits to practice magic or sorcery

Note that in today's society, Harry Potter has become very popular. Harry Potter is a rebellious boy who is enrolled in advancement training for witches and warlocks. He practices sorcery. Unfortunately, our culture is enjoying Harry Potter books and movies even though they are centered around a subject that God has forbidden. We are called to glorify God, not entertain ourselves with the enemy's forbidden fruits.

*Acts 13:8*
*8 But Elymas the sorcerer (for so his name is translated) withstood them, seeking to turn the proconsul away from the faith.*
*9 Then Saul, who also is called Paul, filled with the Holy Spirit, looked intently at him*
*10 and said, "O full of all deceit and all fraud, you son of the devil, you enemy of all righteousness, will you not cease perverting the straight ways of the Lord?"*

*Revelations 22:15*
*15 But outside are dogs and sorcerers and sexually immoral and murderers and idolaters, and whoever loves and practices a lie.*

## WITCHES

Those who practice sorcery
(A wizard is a male witch.)

*Deuteronomy 18:10*
*10 There shall not be found among you anyone who makes his son or*
*his daughter pass through the fire, or one who practices witchcraft, or a*
*soothsayer, or one who interprets omens, or a sorcerer.*

## The Second List
## Notable religions that are directly anti-God in nature

**Shintoist:** Primarily a system of nature and ancestor worship

**Shivaist:** People who worship the god Shiva the Destroyer. Shiva is the third member of the trimurti, along with Brahma the creator and Vishnu the preserver.

**Hinduist:** Those who participate in any of the various forms of modified Brahmanism with additions of Buddhitic and other religious and philosophic idea. It is the religion and social system of the Hindus

**Buddhist:** A religion and philosophic system of central and eastern Asia, founded in India in the sixth century B.C. by Buddha. It teaches that right living, right thinking, and self-denial will enable the soul to reach Nirvana, a divine state of release from earthly and bodily pain, sorrow, and desire

**Confucianist:** The ethical teaching formulated by Confucius and introduced into the Chinese religion, emphasizing devotion to parents, family, and friends, ancestor worship, and the maintenance of justice and peace.

## The Third List
## Movements opposed to Jesus Christ as Lord

The next list includes movements that started after the Bible was written. Those in this list have direct ties to anti-God teachings.

Note: Some of the following movements have intentionally lied to their members about the identity of the god they mention during their meetings. Any of you who have been involved in these movements with or without knowledge of their ungodly teachings need to repent from involvement in these organizations and leave them. There are many fine books at Christian bookstores to help you with any specific questions you have about these organizations.

**New Age teachers:** These are people who frequently form groups that have at their very core the teachings of ancient mysticism. They use old techniques and attempt to make them appear new and attractive. These include Egyptology, sorcery, scientology, and other belief systems of old, but recently they have given these old practices new names and added additional thoughts in order to appear modern and attractive.

**Nation of Islam or Muslims:** These are people who follow the religious faith of Muslims, as set forth in the Koran. The Koran teaches that Allah is the only God and that Muhammad is his prophet. The Koran clearly states that Allah has NO SON.

*Another definition is the whole body of Muslim believers, their civilization, and the countries in which theirs is the dominant religion.*

**Masonic orders or Freemason members:** These are members of a widely-distributed secret order. Their goal is mutual assistance and the promotion of brotherly love among its members. It originated as a medieval society composed of skilled stoneworkers. Today, this movement pretends to be a godly organization, yet those who attain the level of 32$^{nd}$ Mason find that the god the masons have worshiped is Lucifer (Satan).

**Order of the Eastern Star:** Dr. Rob Morris began the Order of the Eastern Star. He was a mason and wrote many books which are used as references in Masonic libraries. He thought that Masonry should be open to women and this was the reason that he started this organization. The Order of the Eastern Star is open to men who are Masons and women who have specific Masonic affiliation.

**Mormons:** These are members of the Church of Jesus Christ of Latter-Day Saints, founded in the United States in 1830 by Joseph Smith. Mormons believe that God was once a man, and he became a god and then got his own planet. The desire of the male members of the Mormon Church is to one day be a god and have their own planet. In their religion, Jesus and Lucifer are brothers. Their god is not the God of the Bible, even though they claim to believe the King James Version of the Bible. Note that when the King James Version of the Bible and their beliefs differ, the leadership of the Mormon Church tells their members to disregard the authority of the King James Version of the Bible.

**Jehovah's Witnesses:** This is a sect founded by Charles T. Russell in the United States in the 19$^{th}$ century. Russell predicted that the world would end in 1914. Members of the group do not believe in the trinity. They do not believe that Jesus is the eternal God, but instead that he was the first creation of God. In their literature, they say that Jesus lived in heaven as a spirit person before he came to earth. In addition, they teach that Jesus was called Michael the Archangel before he was born on earth. *The Watchtower* is their magazine.

**Darwinists:** These are people who believe in the Darwinian Theory of Evolution. Darwin said that life came from nonliving things over a period of millions of years.

**Communism:** The political system of communism elevates the state above individual rights. In the communist governments of the recent decades, we have seen a definite defiance against God. Those citizens who become Christians, or even become curious about Christianity, are persecuted.

**Stalinism:** The political theories and practices of Josef Stalin (1879-1953), premier and marshal of the Soviet Union. They worshiped him.

**Satanists:** These are people who worship the devil and seek to gain power from him.

**All involved in the occult:** The word "occult" means hidden or secret things. Those in the occult use certain mystic arts or studies. They are tapping into occult forces and powers.

**All cultists:** People who are in cults.

**The Fourth List**
**Categories of people headed for hell**

The next list contains people whose sins are specifically spelled out as sins. These are sins that those who are headed toward hell will display. As you read the scriptures, you will also see some sins that are not highlighted in this book but nevertheless are contained in the scriptures.

## LIARS

*Revelation 21:8, 27*
*8 "But the cowardly, unbelieving, abominable, murderers, sexually immoral, sorcerers, idolaters, and all liars shall have their part in the lake which burns with fire and brimstone, which is the second death."*
*27 "But there shall by no means enter it anything that defiles, or causes an abomination or a lie, but only those who are written in the Lamb's Book of Life."*

*I John 2:4*
*4 He who says, "I know Him," and does not keep His commandments, is a liar, and the truth is not in him.*

## HOMOSEXUALS AND LESBIANS

Sexual actions towards a member of one's own sex

*Romans 1:20-32*
*20 For since the creation of the world His invisible attributes are clearly seen, being understood by the things that are made, even His eternal power and Godhead, so that they are without excuse,*
*21 because, although they knew God, they did not glorify Him as God, nor were thankful, but became futile in their thoughts, and their foolish hearts were darkened.*

*22 Professing to be wise, they became fools,*

*23 and changed the glory of the incorruptible God into an image made like corruptible man and birds and four-footed beasts and creeping things.*

*24 Therefore God also gave them up to uncleanness, in the lusts of their hearts, to dishonor their bodies among themselves,*

*25 who exchanged the truth of God for the lie, and worshiped and served the creature rather than the Creator, who is blessed forever. Amen.*

*26 For this reason God gave them up to vile passions. For even their women exchanged the natural use for what is against nature.*

*27 Likewise also the men, leaving the natural use of the woman, burned in their lust for one another, men with men committing what is shameful, and receiving in themselves the penalty of their error which was due.*

*28 And even as they did not like to retain God in their knowledge, God gave them over to a debased mind, to do those things which are not fitting;*

*29 being filled with all unrighteousness, sexual immorality, wickedness, covetousness, maliciousness; full of envy, murder, strife, deceit, evil-mindedness; they are whisperers,*

*30 backbiters, haters of God, violent, proud, boasters, inventors of evil things, disobedient to parents,*

*31 undiscerning, untrustworthy, unloving, unforgiving, unmerciful;*

*32 who, knowing the righteous judgment of God, that those who practice such things are deserving of death, not only do the same but also approve of those who practice them.*

## EFFIMINATE

Men having feminine qualities inappropriate to a man

*1 Corinthians 6:9*

*9 Do you not know that the unrighteous will not inherit the kingdom of God? Do not be deceived. Neither fornicators, nor idolaters, nor adulterers, nor homosexuals, nor sodomites. . .*

## WHOREMONGER
Those who consort with prostitutes

*Revelation 21:8 KJV*
*8 But the fearful, and unbelieving, and the abominable, and murderers, and whoremongers, and sorcerers, and idolaters, and all liars, shall have their part in the lake which burneth with fire and brimstone: which is the second death.*

## UNGODLY
Those who have a disregard for God's truth

*Jude 1:14-15*
*14 Now Enoch, the seventh from Adam, prophesied about these men also, saying, "Behold, the Lord comes with ten thousands of His saints,*
*15 to execute judgment on all, to convict all who are ungodly among them of all their ungodly deeds which they have committed in an ungodly way, and of all the harsh things which ungodly sinners have spoken against Him."*

## FEARFUL/ COWARDLY

The Greek word is "deos." It stands for two of our words. The definition of "deos" includes the understanding of our word "timid" and also our word "fearful." It is interpreted as those who have feelings of fear, dread, or apprehension, or those who fear others more than they fear God. We see in this word the concept of lacking courage or contemptibly timid.

Notice that some Bible translations choose to translate the Greek word as "fearful" and some as "cowardly."

*Revelation 21:8 KJV*
8 *"But the fearful, and unbelieving, and the abominable, and murderers, and whoremongers, and sorcerers, and idolaters, and all liars, shall have their part in the lake which burneth with fire and brimstone: which is the second death."*

*Revelation 21:8*
8 *"But the cowardly, unbelieving, abominable, murderers, sexually immoral, sorcerers, idolaters, and all liars shall have their part in the lake which burns with fire and brimstone, which is the second death."*

## UNRIGHTEOUS

Those who are not justified before God; those who are sinful; wicked

*2 Thessalonians 2:11-12*
11 *And for this reason God will send them strong delusion, that they should believe the lie,*
12 *that they all may be condemned who did not believe the truth but had pleasure in unrighteousness.*

## SUPPRESSORS OF TRUTH IN UNRIGHTEOUSNESS

*Roman 1:18*
18 *For the wrath of God is revealed from heaven against all ungodliness and unrighteousness of men, who suppress the truth in unrighteousness. . .*

## FOOLS

One deficient in good sense or judgment; one who can easily be duped

*Luke 12:20*
20 "But God said to him, 'Fool! This night your soul will be required of you; then whose will those things be which you have provided?'"

## FOOLISH

## Those who misuse wisdom

*Matthew 25:1-13*
1 "Then the kingdom of heaven shall be likened to ten virgins who took their lamps and went out to meet the bridegroom.
2 Now five of them were wise, and five were foolish.
3 Those who were foolish took their lamps and took no oil with them,
4 but the wise took oil in their vessels with their lamps.
5 But while the bridegroom was delayed, they all slumbered and slept."
6 "And at midnight a cry was heard: 'Behold, the bridegroom is coming; go out to meet him!'
7 Then all those virgins arose and trimmed their lamps.
8 And the foolish said to the wise, 'Give us some of your oil, for our lamps are going out.'
9 But the wise answered, saying, 'No, lest there should not be enough for us and you; but go rather to those who sell, and buy for yourselves.'
10 And while they went to buy, the bridegroom came, and those who were ready went in with him to the wedding; and the door was shut."
11 "Afterward the other virgins came also, saying, 'Lord, Lord, open to us!'
12 But he answered and said, 'Assuredly, I say to you, I do not know you.'
13 "Watch therefore, for you know neither the day nor the hour in which the Son of Man is coming."

## UNWORTHY

Those not being fit; lacking merit

All are unworthy unless they have been made righteous by the blood of Jesus. We must accept the sacrifice of Jesus and worship Him as Lord in order to be counted worthy. We are made right through Christ. (After salvation, we receive the armor of righteousness; it is the armor of our Savior Jesus. See Ephesians 6:14.)

*Acts 13:46*
*46 Then Paul and Barnabas grew bold and said, "It was necessary that the word of God should be spoken to you first; but since you reject it, and judge yourselves unworthy of everlasting life, behold, we turn to the Gentiles."*

## LOST

Those who are blinded by Satan; they are the unsaved

*2 Corinthians 4:3-4 KJV*
*3 But if our gospel be hid, it is hid to them that are lost:*
*4 In whom the god of this world hath blinded the minds of them which believe not, lest the light of the glorious gospel of Christ, who is the image of God, should shine unto them.*

## UNFORGIVING

Those who refuse to forgive others

*Matthew 6:14-15*
*14 "For if you forgive men their trespasses, your heavenly Father will also forgive you.*
*15 But if you do not forgive men their trespasses, neither will your Father forgive your trespasses."*

## UNMERCIFUL

Those who will not show mercy to others

*James 2:13*
*13 For judgment is without mercy to the one who has shown no mercy.*
*Mercy triumphs over judgment.*

## DARKNESS

Those who are ignorant; moral or spiritual destitution

*Ephesians 5:7-8, 11*
*7 Therefore do not be partakers with them.*
*8 For you were once darkness, but now you are light in the Lord. Walk*
*as children of light. . .*
*11 And have no fellowship with the unfruitful works of darkness, but*
*rather expose them.*

## WORKERS of WITCHCRAFT

Those who practice sorcery

*Galatians 5:19-20 KJV*
*19 Now the works of the flesh are manifest, which are these; Adultery,*
*fornication, uncleanness, lasciviousness,*
*20 Idolatry, witchcraft, hatred, variance, emulations, wrath, strife, sedi-*
*tions, heresies,*

## WORKERS OF THE FLESH

*Galatians 5:19-21*
*19 Now the works of the flesh are evident, which are: adultery, fornica-*
*tion, uncleanness, lewdness,*

*20 idolatry, sorcery, hatred, contentions, jealousies, outbursts of wrath, selfish ambitions, dissensions, heresies,*
*21 envy, murders, drunkenness, revelries, and the like; of which I tell you beforehand, just as I also told you in time past, that those who practice such things will not inherit the kingdom of God*

## FORNICATORS

Those who are unmarried and have sexual relations with each other

*Ephesians 5:5*
*5 For this you know, that no fornicator, unclean person, nor covetous man, who is an idolater, has any inheritance in the kingdom of Christ and God.*

## ADULTERERS

Those who have sexual relations with someone other than their own spouse

*Hebrews 13:4*
*4 Marriage is honorable among all, and the bed undefiled; but fornicators and adulterers God will judge.*

## PERJURERS

Those who have sworn falsely

*1 Timothy 1:9-10*
*9 knowing this: that the law is not made for a righteous person, but for the lawless and insubordinate, for the ungodly and for sinners, for the unholy and profane, for murderers of fathers and murderers of mothers, for manslayers,*

*10 for fornicators, for sodomites, for kidnappers, for liars, for perjurers, and if there is any other thing that is contrary to sound doctrine,*

## IDOLATERS

Those who worship idols or people

*I Corinthians 6:9*
*9 Do you not know that the unrighteous will not inherit the kingdom of God? Do not be deceived. Neither fornicators, nor idolaters, nor adulterers, nor homosexuals, nor sodomites,*

## COVETERS

Those who have an insatiable desire for worldly gain

*I Corinthians 6:9-10*
*9 Do you not know that the unrighteous will not inherit the kingdom of God? Do not be deceived. Neither fornicators, nor idolaters, nor adulterers, nor homosexuals, nor sodomites,*
*10 nor thieves, nor covetous, nor drunkards, nor revilers, nor extortioners will inherit the kingdom of God.*

## FILTHY

Those with uncleanliness, defilement, corruption

*Revelation 22:11-12*
*11 "He who is unjust, let him be unjust still; he who is filthy, let him be filthy still; he who is righteous, let him be righteous still; he who is holy, let him be holy still."*
*12 "And behold, I am coming quickly, and My reward is with Me, to give to every one according to his work."*

## LEWD

Those who are wicked, salacious, licentious

*Ezekiel 23:46-49*
*46 "For thus says the Lord God: 'Bring up an assembly against them, give them up to trouble and plunder.*
*47 The assembly shall stone them with stones and execute them with their swords; they shall slay their sons and their daughters, and burn their houses with fire.*
*48 Thus I will cause lewdness to cease from the land, that all women may be taught not to practice your lewdness.*
*49 They shall repay you for your lewdness, and you shall pay for your idolatrous sins. Then you shall know that I am the Lord God.'"*

## WORKERS OF ABOMINATION

Those who do things utterly repulsive to God

*Revelation 21:27 KJV*
*7 And there shall in no wise enter into it any thing that defileth, neither whatsoever worketh abomination, or maketh a lie: but they which are written in the Lamb's Book of Life.*

## MURDERERS

Those who kill unlawfully

*Revelation 22:15 KJV*
*15 For without are dogs, and sorcerers, and whoremongers, and murderers, and idolaters, and whosoever loveth and maketh a lie.*

## SEXUALLY IMMORAL

Those who practice sexual contact condemned in scripture

*Revelation 22:15*
*15 But outside are dogs and sorcerers and sexually immoral and murderers and idolaters, and whoever loves and practices a lie.*

## SODOMITES

Those who practice sodomy

*1 Corinthians 6:9*
*9 Do you not know that the unrighteous will not inherit the kingdom of God? Do not be deceived. Neither fornicators, nor idolaters, nor adulterers, nor homosexuals, nor sodomites,*

## UNCLEAN PERSON

Someone who is evil or vile or corrupt

*Ephesians 5:5*
*5 For this you know, that no fornicator, unclean person, nor covetous man, who is an idolater, has any inheritance in the kingdom of Christ and God.*

## EXTORTIONERS

Those who wrongfully take money or property from others by threat of violence

*1 Corinthians 6:10*
*10 nor thieves, nor covetous, nor drunkards, nor revilers, nor extortioners, will inherit the kingdom of God.*

## UNJUST

Those characterized by injustice

*Revelation 22:11*
*11 "He who is unjust, let him be unjust still; he who is filthy, let him be
filthy still; he who is righteous, let him be righteous still; he who is holy,
let him be holy still."*

## UNHOLY

Those who are wicked; those showing disregard for holiness

*2 Timothy 3:2*
*2 For men will be lovers of themselves, lovers of money, boasters, proud,
blasphemers, disobedient to parents, unthankful, unholy,*

## DECEIVERS

Those who mislead others

*2 John 1:7*
*7 "For many deceivers have gone out into the world who do not confess
Jesus Christ as coming in the flesh. This is a deceiver and an antichrist."*

## DISOBEDIENT

Those who rebel against recognized authority

*Ephesians 5:6*
*6 "Let no one deceive you with empty words, for because of these things
the wrath of God comes upon the sons of disobedience."*

## THOSE WITH HARDNESS OF HEART

*Romans 2:5-9*

*5 But in accordance with your hardness and your impenitent heart you are treasuring up for yourself wrath in the day of wrath and revelation of the righteous judgment of God,*

*6 who "will render to each one according to his deeds"*

*7 eternal life to those who by patient continuance in doing good seek for glory, honor, and immortality;*

*8 but to those who are self-seeking and do not obey the truth, but obey unrighteousness—indignation and wrath,*

*9 tribulation and anguish, on every soul of man who does evil, of the Jew first and also of the Greek;*

## SON OF HELL

*Matthew 23:14-15, 33*

*14 "Woe to you, scribes and Pharisees, hypocrites! For you devour widow' houses, and for a pretense make long prayers. Therefore you will receive greater condemnation."*

*15 "Woe to you, scribes and Pharisees, hypocrites! For you travel land and sea to win one proselyte, and when he is won, you make him twice as much a son of hell as yourselves."*

*33 "Serpents, brood of vipers! How can you escape the condemnation of hell?"*

## ANGRY PEOPLE

*Matthew 5:22, 29-30*

*22 "But I say to you that whoever is angry with his brother without a cause shall be in danger of the judgment. And whoever says to his brother, 'Raca!' shall be in danger of the council. But whoever says, 'You fool!' shall be in danger of hell fire."*

*29 "If your right eye causes you to sin, pluck it out and cast it from you; for it is more profitable for you that one of your members perish, than for your whole body to be cast into hell."*

*30 "And if your right hand causes you to sin, cut it off and cast it from you; for it is more profitable for you that one of your members perish, than for your whole body to be cast into hell."*

## DOGS

Those who are unsaved

At the time of Jesus, the word "dogs" was a term used for heathens (or Gentiles).

*Revelation 22:15*
*15 But outside are dogs and sorcerers and sexually immoral and murderers and idolaters, and whoever loves and practices a lie.*

## PAGANISM IN THE CHURCH—JEZEBEL

*Revelation 2:18-24*
*18 "And to the angel of the church in Thyatira write, 'These things says the Son of God, who has eyes like a flame of fire, and His feet like fine brass:*

*19 I know your works, love, service, faith, and your patience; and as for your works, the last are more than the first.*

*20 Nevertheless I have a few things against you, because you allow that woman Jezebel, who calls herself a prophetess, to teach and seduce My servants to commit sexual immorality and eat things sacrificed to idols.*

*21 And I gave her time to repent of her sexual immorality, and she did not repent.*

*22 Indeed I will cast her into a sickbed, and those who commit adultery with her into great tribulation, unless they repent of their deeds.*

*23 And I will kill her children with death, and all the churches shall know that I am He who searches the minds and hearts. And I will give to each one of you according to your works."*

*24 "Now to you I say, and to the rest in Thyatira, as many as do not have this doctrine, who have not known the depths of Satan, as they say, I will put on you no other burden."'*

## NICOLATIONS

Those who were part of an early Christian sect group teaching moral looseness

*Revelation 2:15-16*
*15 "Thus you also have those who hold the doctrine of the Nicolaitans, which thing I hate.*
*16 Repent, or else I will come to you quickly and will fight against them with the sword of My mouth."*

## THOSE WHO ARE NOT IN THE LAMB'S BOOK OF LIFE

*Revelation 21:27*
*27 But there shall by no means enter it anything that defiles, or causes an abomination or a lie, but only those who are written in the Lamb's Book of Life.*

## THE WICKED

Those who are evil; disposed to wrongdoing; vile

*Psalm 9:16-17*
*16 "The Lord is known by the judgment He executes; The wicked is snared in the work of his own hands. Meditation. Selah"*

17 *"The wicked shall be turned into hell, And all the nations that forget God."*

*Psalms 55:15*
15 *Let death seize upon them; Let them go down alive into hell, For wickedness is in their dwellings and among them.*

## UNSAVED

Those who are without Christ as Savior

*Luke 13:23-24*
23 *Then one said to Him, "Lord, are there few who are saved?" And He said to them,*
24 *"Strive to enter through the narrow gate, for many, I say to you, will seek to enter and will not be able."*

## UNBELIEVERS

Those who are not Christians

*Revelation 21:8*
8 *"But the cowardly, unbelieving, abominable, murderers, sexually im-moral, sorcerers, idolaters, and all liars shall have their part in the lake which burns with fire and brimstone, which is the second death."*

## THOSE WHO NEVER KNEW THE LORD

Jesus teaches that some people will call him, "Lord," but not be true believers.

*Matthew 7:19-23*
19 *"Every tree that does not bear good fruit is cut down and thrown into the fire.*

*20 Therefore by their fruits you will know them."*

*21 "Not everyone who says to Me, 'Lord, Lord,' shall enter the kingdom of heaven, but he who does the will of My Father in heaven.*

*22 Many will say to Me in that day, 'Lord, Lord, have we not prophesied in Your name, cast out demons in Your name, and done many wonders in Your name?'*

*23 And then I will declare to them, 'I never knew you; depart from Me, you who practice lawlessness!'"*

## FINAL WARNING from GOD:
## All who do not accept salvation from the God of the Bible are going to an eternal hell.

*1 John 2:23-26*

*23 Whoever denies the Son does not have the Father either; he who acknowledges the Son has the Father also.*

*24 Therefore let that abide in you which you heard from the beginning. If what you heard from the beginning abides in you, you also will abide in the Son and in the Father.*

*25 And this is the promise that He has promised us—eternal life.*

*26 These things I have written to you concerning those who try to deceive you.*

# GOD THE FATHER, JESUS, THE HOLY SPIRIT, AND HELL

## THE PRESENCE OF THE LORD

God is omnipresent. That means He is present everywhere. Therefore, the Lord can see those who are in hell.

*Psalm 139:7-8*
*7 Where can I go from Your Spirit? Or where can I flee from Your presence?*
*8 If I ascend into heaven, You are there; If I make my bed in hell, behold, You are there.*

## BEFORE THE LORD

*Proverbs 15:8-11, 15,24*
*8 The sacrifice of the wicked is an abomination to the Lord, But the prayer of the upright is His delight.*
*9 The way of the wicked is an abomination to the Lord, But He loves him who follows righteousness.*
*10 Harsh discipline is for him who forsakes the way, And he who hates correction will die.*
*11 Hell and Destruction are before the Lord; So how much more the hearts of the sons of men.*
*15 All the days of the afflicted are evil, But he who is of a merry heart has a continual feast.*
*24 The way of life winds upward for the wise, That he may turn away from hell below.*

## GOD HAS POWER TO CAST PEOPLE INTO

*Luke 12:5*
*5 "But I will show you whom you should fear: Fear Him who, after He has killed, has power to cast into hell; yes, I say to you, fear Him!"*

## GOD SENDS SOUL AND BODY TO DESTRUCTION IN HELL

*Matthew 10:27-28*

*27 "Whatever I tell you in the dark, speak in the light; and what you hear in the ear, preach on the housetops.*
*28 And do not fear those who kill the body but cannot kill the soul. But rather fear Him who is able to destroy both soul and body in hell."*

## JESUS WENT THERE

Jesus went to hell after He was crucified.

*Ephesians 4:8-10*
*8 Therefore He says: "When he ascended on high, He led captivity captive, And gave gifts to men."*
*9 (Now this, "He ascended"—what does it mean but that He also first descended into the lower parts of the earth?*
*10 He who descended is also the One who ascended far above all the heavens, that He might fill all things.)*

## YOU WILL NOT LEAVE MY SOUL IN HELL [Jesus is speaking.]

These are verses that explain that Jesus will not stay in hell.

*Psalms 16:7-10 KJV*

7 I will bless the LORD, who hath given me counsel: my reins also instruct me in the night seasons.

8 I have set the LORD always before me: because he is at my right hand, I shall not be moved.

9 Therefore my heart is glad, and my glory rejoiceth: my flesh also shall rest in hope.

10 For thou wilt not leave my soul in hell; neither wilt thou suffer thine Holy One to see corruption.

*Acts 2:27 KJV*

27 Because thou wilt not leave my soul in hell, neither wilt thou suffer thine Holy One to see corruption.

## JESUS HAS THE KEY TO HELL AND DEATH

*Revelation 1:18 KJV*

18 "I am he that liveth, and was dead; and, behold, I am alive for evermore, Amen; and have the keys of hell and of death."

## JESUS CAN SEND YOU THERE

*Luke 3:9, 16-17*

9 "And even now the ax is laid to the root of the trees. Therefore every tree which does not bear good fruit is cut down and thrown into the fire."

16 John answered, saying to all, "I indeed baptize you with water; but One mightier than I is coming, whose sandal strap I am not worthy to loose. He will baptize you with the Holy Spirit and fire.

17 His winnowing fan is in His hand, and He will thoroughly clean out His threshing floor, and gather the wheat into His barn; but the chaff He will burn with unquenchable fire."

*John 15:6*

6 "If anyone does not abide in Me, he is cast out as a branch and is

*withered; and they gather them and throw them into the fire, and they are burned."*

*Jude 1:3-23*

*3 Beloved, while I was very diligent to write to you concerning our common salvation, I found it necessary to write to you exhorting you to contend earnestly for the faith which was once for all delivered to the saints.*

*4 For certain men have crept in unnoticed, who long ago were marked out for this condemnation, ungodly men, who turn the grace of our God into lewdness and deny the only Lord God and our Lord Jesus Christ.*

*5 But I want to remind you, though you once knew this, that the Lord, having saved the people out of the land of Egypt, afterward destroyed those who did not believe.*

*6 And the angels who did not keep their proper domain, but left their own abode, He has reserved in everlasting chains under darkness for the judgment of the great day;*

*7 as Sodom and Gomorrah, and the cities around them in a similar manner to these, having given themselves over to sexual immorality and gone after strange flesh, are set forth as an example, suffering the vengeance of eternal fire.*

*8 Likewise also these dreamers defile the flesh, reject authority, and speak evil of dignitaries.*

*9 Yet Michael the archangel, in contending with the devil, when he disputed about the body of Moses, dared not bring against him a reviling accusation, but said, "The Lord rebuke you!"*

*10 But these speak evil of whatever they do not know; and whatever they know naturally, like brute beasts, in these things they corrupt themselves.*

*11 Woe to them! For they have gone in the way of Cain, have run greedily in the error of Balaam for profit, and perished in the rebellion of Korah.*

*12 These are spots in your love feasts, while they feast with you without fear, serving only themselves. They are clouds without water, carried about by the winds; late autumn trees without fruit, twice dead, pulled up by the roots;*

13 *raging waves of the sea, foaming up their own shame; wandering stars for whom is reserved the blackness of darkness forever.*

14 *Now Enoch, the seventh from Adam, prophesied about these men also, saying, "Behold, the Lord comes with ten thousands of His saints,*

15 *to execute judgment on all, to convict all who are ungodly among them of all their ungodly deeds which they have committed in an ungodly way, and of all the harsh things which ungodly sinners have spoken against Him."*

16 *These are grumblers, complainers, walking according to their own lusts; and they mouth great swelling words, flattering people to gain advantage.*

17 *But you, beloved, remember the words which were spoken before by the apostles of our Lord Jesus Christ:*

18 *how they told you that there would be mockers in the last time who would walk according to their own ungodly lusts.*

19 *These are sensual persons, who cause divisions, not having the Spirit.*

20 *But you, beloved, building yourselves up on your most holy faith, praying in the Holy Spirit,*

21 *keep yourselves in the love of God, looking for the mercy of our Lord Jesus Christ unto eternal life.*

22 *And on some have compassion, making a distinction;*

23 *but others save with fear, pulling them out of the fire, hating even the garment defiled by the flesh.*

## SPIRIT OF TRUTH TESTIFIES TO THE TRUTH OF HELL AND OF THE GOSPEL OF LIFE

*John 16:13*

13 *"However, when He, the Spirit of truth, has come, He will guide you into all truth; for He will not speak on His own authority, but whatever He hears He will speak; and He will tell you things to come."*

## MORE FACTS ABOUT HELL

This chapter will uncover more information about hell. In addition, this chapter will include God's strong plea to people to stay away from hell.

### NEVER FULL

*Proverb 27:20*
*20 Hell and Destruction are never full; So the eyes of man are never satisfied.*

### ENLARGED

*Isaiah 5:14 KJV*
*14 Therefore hell hath enlarged herself, and opened her mouth without measure: and their glory, and their multitude, and their pomp, and he that rejoiceth, shall descend into it.*

### COMPARED TO A MAN AND ENLARGED

*Habakkuk 2:5*
*5 "Indeed, because he transgresses by wine, He is a proud man, and he does not stay at home. Because he enlarges his desire as hell, and he is like death, and cannot be satisfied, He gathers to himself all nations And heaps up for himself all peoples."*

### HELL IS ANCIENT

Hell existed before Genesis 1:1.

*Genesis 1:1*
*1 In the beginning God created the heavens and the earth.*

## JESUS TELLS ABOUT A PERSON IN HELL

In Luke 16:19, Jesus tells a lengthy story about a poor man named Lazarus and a rich man who is unnamed. The rich man dies and goes to hell. Lazarus dies and goes to Abraham's bosom. The term "Abraham's bosom " is a term that signifies paradise.

The story not only tells of the horror of hell but it also gives an inherent cry to all who hear it to heed its warnings and turn to the one who gives eternal life.

*Luke 16:19-31*
*19 "There was a certain rich man who was clothed in purple and fine linen and fared sumptuously every day.*
*20 But there was a certain beggar named Lazarus, full of sores, who was laid at his gate,*
*21 desiring to be fed with the crumbs which fell from the rich man's table. Moreover the dogs came and licked his sores.*
*22 So it was that the beggar died, and was carried by the angels to Abraham's bosom. The rich man also died and was buried.*
*23 And being in torments in Hades, he lifted up his eyes and saw Abraham afar off, and Lazarus in his bosom."*
*24 "Then he cried and said, 'Father Abraham, have mercy on me, and send Lazarus that he may dip the tip of his finger in water and cool my tongue; for I am tormented in this flame.'*
*25 But Abraham said, 'Son, remember that in your lifetime you received your good things, and likewise Lazarus evil things; but now he is comforted and you are tormented.*
*26 And besides all this, between us and you there is a great gulf fixed, so that those who want to pass from here to you cannot, nor can those from there pass to us.'"*

*27 "Then he said, 'I beg you therefore, father, that you would send him to my father's house,*
*28 for I have five brothers, that he may testify to them, lest they also come to this place of torment.'*
*29 Abraham said to him, 'They have Moses and the prophets; let them hear them.'*
*30 And he said, 'No, father Abraham; but if one goes to them from the dead, they will repent.'*
*31 But he said to him, 'If they do not hear Moses and the prophets, neither will they be persuaded though one rise from the dead.'"*

## MANY STRONG AND MIGHTY PEOPLE WILL BE IN HELL

Some people think that if a person is strong and powerful enough, rich enough, or famous enough then that person will be able to escape hell. The truth is that those who are mighty **and** those who are weak will be in hell if they do not accept Jesus as their Lord.

*Ezekiel 32:21*
*21 "The strong among the mighty Shall speak to him out of the midst of hell With those who help him: 'They have gone down, They lie with the uncircumcised, slain by the sword.'"*

## THERE IS NO ESCAPE FROM HELL

No one, no matter how powerful or intelligent, can escape from the judgment of God. There is no limit to God's awareness and no limit to his power. He would know if someone was trying to hide in hell or trying to break into heaven.

*Amos 9:2*
2 *"Though they dig into hell, From there My hand shall take them; Though they climb up to heaven, From there I will bring them down;"*

## HELL WILL NOT PREVAIL AGAINST THE CHURCH

*Matthew 16:18 KJV*
18 *"And I say also unto thee, That thou art Peter, and upon this rock I will build my church; and the gates of hell shall not prevail against it."*

## WHAT HELL IS NOT !

Many in today's media would have you think that hell will be a place of parties and fun. They paint a picture of people enjoying a life of leisure. Nevertheless, nothing could be farther from the truth. Hell is not a playground or an amusement park. It is a place of moment-by-moment torment that continues forever.

FOREVER is a long time!

## THE MYTH OF REINCARNATION

Some people like to think that they can keep coming back to earth in a different body. The term for that belief is "reincarnation." The Bible is clear that reincarnation is a false belief.

*Hebrews 9:27*
27 And as it is appointed for men to die once, but after this the judgment.

## THOSE WHO CALL HELL A FABLE

Some false religions and some individual people teach that there is no hell. They believe that everyone goes to heaven or that everyone just goes to an eternal sleep. Anyone who believes one of those lies is in essence saying that the God of the Bible is lying.

The Story of Elijah

Elijah was an Old Testament prophet. He was confronted with people who did not believe God and his words. So Elijah confronted the prophets of the false god Baal.

> *1 Kings 18:18-21*
>
> *18 And he [Elijah] answered, "I have not troubled Israel, but you and your father's house have, in that you have forsaken the commandments of the Lord and have followed the Baals.*
>
> *19 Now therefore, send and gather all Israel to me on Mount Carmel, the four hundred and fifty prophets of Baal, and the four hundred prophets of Asherah, who eat at Jezebel's table."*
>
> *20 So Ahab sent for all the children of Israel, and gathered the prophets together on Mount Carmel.*
>
> *21 And Elijah came to all the people, and said, "How long will you falter between two opinions? If the Lord is God, follow Him; but if Baal, follow him."*

The story continues as Elijah announces a contest. Each side was to have a sacrifice. The winning team would have their sacrifice consumed by its god (God). Everyone waited for hours for Baal to do something. Baal did nothing. Then Elijah got his sacrifice ready. He poured so much water over his bull sacrifice that it filled up a trench that was dug around the altar. When Elijah called upon God the miraculous happened.

> *1 Kings 18:38-39*
>
> *38 Then the fire of the Lord fell and consumed the burnt sacrifice, and the wood and the stones and the dust, and it licked up the water that was in the trench.*
>
> *39 Now when all the people saw it, they fell on their faces; and they said, "The Lord, He is God! The Lord, He is God!"*

Therefore, I challenge you, the reader. If God is God, follow him.

I hope you will now rejoice with me that, "The Lord, He is God! The Lord, He is God!"

## WARNINGS FROM GOD

God gives many specific warnings that are aimed at alerting us to the seriousness of our choices in life. Bad choices will eventually cause pain and heartache in this life, yet their eternal consequences are even more serious. The bad choices we make can lead us straight down the path to hell. It is important to remember that there is a heaven that can be missed and a hell that can be experienced. There is the certainty of hell in the next life if God's warnings are shunned. Without repentance, our future destination is hell.

### CHOOSE CAREFULLY

God gives us the responsibility to make choices. We decide if we will make good choices or bad choices.

*Deuteronomy 30:15-18*
*15 "See, I have set before you today life and good, death and evil,*
*16 in that I command you today to love the Lord your God, to walk in His ways, and to keep His commandments, His statutes, and His judgments, that you may live and multiply; and the Lord your God will bless you in the land which you go to possess.*
*17 But if your heart turns away so that you do not hear, and are drawn away, and worship other gods and serve them,*
*18 I announce to you today that you shall surely perish;"*

God has warnings for many specific circumstances. This chapter will not contain all of the warnings of God; however, there will be information on the following warnings:

Beware of ignoring or despising Bible scriptures.
Beware of being ashamed of the Lord.
Beware of ungodly companions.
Beware of the love of money.
Beware of pride.
Beware of fornication.
Beware of adultery.
Beware of pornography.
Beware of prostitutes.
Beware of the prostitution business.
Beware of downplaying hell.
Beware of your words.
Beware of neglecting to discipline your children.
Beware of abusing children.
Beware of rejecting wisdom.
Beware of ignoring godly correction.
Beware of covering your sins.

## BEWARE OF IGNORING OR DESPISING BIBLE SCRIPTURES

God has given us the Bible in order to teach us and inform us.

*Proverbs 13:13-14*
*13 He who despises the word will be destroyed, But he who fears the commandment will be rewarded.*
*14 The law of the wise is a fountain of life, To turn one away from the snares of death.*

In Luke 16:19, Jesus tells us a story about a poor man named Lazarus and a rich man who is unnamed. The rich man dies and goes to hell, and Lazarus dies and goes to Abraham's bosom. (The term "Abraham's bosom " is a term that signifies paradise.) In the story, it is clear that those who do not heed the warnings of scripture will be facing an eternity of hell. Therefore, inherent in these scriptures is the cry of the Lord to us to spend time in the Bible and take seriously His words to us.

*Luke 16:19-31*
*19 "There was a certain rich man who was clothed in purple and fine linen and fared sumptuously every day.*
*20 But there was a certain beggar named Lazarus, full of sores, who was laid at his gate,*
*21 desiring to be fed with the crumbs which fell from the rich man's table. Moreover the dogs came and licked his sores.*
*22 So it was that the beggar died, and was carried by the angels to Abraham's bosom. The rich man also died and was buried.*
*23 And being in torments in Hades, he lifted up his eyes and saw Abraham afar off, and Lazarus in his bosom."*
*24 "Then he cried and said, 'Father Abraham, have mercy on me, and send Lazarus that he may dip the tip of his finger in water and cool my tongue; for I am tormented in this flame.'*
*25 But Abraham said, 'Son, remember that in your lifetime you received your good things, and likewise Lazarus evil things; but now he is comforted and you are tormented.*
*26 And besides all this, between us and you there is a great gulf fixed, so that those who want to pass from here to you cannot, nor can those from there pass to us.'"*
*27 "Then he said, 'I beg you therefore, father, that you would send him to my father's house,*
*28 for I have five brothers, that he may testify to them, lest they also come to this place of torment.'*
*29 Abraham said to him, 'They have Moses and the prophets; let them hear them.'*
*30 And he said, 'No, father Abraham; but if one goes to them from the dead, they will repent.'*

*31 But he said to him, 'If they do not hear Moses and the prophets, neither will they be persuaded though one rise from the dead.'"*

## BEWARE OF BEING ASHAMED OF THE LORD

*Luke 9:25-26*
*25 "For what profit is it to a man if he gains the whole world, and is himself destroyed or lost?*
*26 For whoever is ashamed of Me and My words, of him the Son of Man will be ashamed when He comes in His own glory, and in His Father's and of the holy angels."*

## BEWARE OF UNGODLY COMPANIONS

*Proverbs 12:26*
*26 The righteous should choose his friends carefully, For the way of the wicked leads them astray.*

*Proverbs 13:20*
*20 He who walks with wise men will be wise, But the companion of fools will be destroyed.*

*Proverbs 22:24-25*
*24 Make no friendship with an angry man, And with a furious man do not go,*
*25 Lest you learn his ways And set a snare for your soul.*

## BEWARE OF THE LOVE OF MONEY

Some people get confused and think that money is evil. It is not money, but the **love** of money that is evil. We are to love God and see money as a blessing of God, a tool to use to do the work of the Lord, and a way to provide for one's family.

*1 Timothy 6:10a*
*10 For the love of money is a root of all kinds of evil.*

## BEWARE OF PRIDE

*Proverbs 16:18*
*18 Pride goes before destruction, And a haughty spirit before a fall.*

## BEWARE OF FORNICATION

*Hebrews 13:4*
*4 Marriage is honorable among all, and the bed undefiled; but fornicators and adulterers God will judge.*

## BEWARE OF ADULTERY

*Proverbs 5:15-20*
*15 Drink water from your own cistern, And running water from your own well.*
*16 Should your fountains be dispersed abroad, Streams of water in the streets?*
*17 Let them be only your own, And not for strangers with you.*
*18 Let your fountain be blessed, And rejoice with the wife of your youth.*
*19 As a loving deer and a graceful doe, Let her breasts satisfy you at all times; And always be enraptured with her love.*
*20 For why should you, my son, be enraptured by an immoral woman, And be embraced in the arms of a seductress?*

*Proverbs 6:27-29*
*27 Can a man take fire to his bosom, And his clothes not be burned?*
*28 Can one walk on hot coals, And his feet not be seared?*
*29 So is he who goes in to his neighbor's wife: Whoever touches her shall not be innocent.*

## BEWARE OF PORNOGRAPHY

One of the new, modern-day versions of prostitution is pornography. In order to produce pornography, someone sinned and sold herself or himself to supply the material OR someone was forced to do it against his or her will. As one reads the next section on prostitutes, one would be wise to realize that pornography IS a form of prostitution.

*Psalm 119:36-37*
*36 Incline my heart to Your testimonies, And not to covetousness,*
*37 Turn away my eyes from looking at worthless things.*

## BEWARE OF PROSTITUTES

In our current world, prostitution is big business. The scriptures clearly warn about the snare of prostitutes. Notice that the Bible says that "her" house is on the way to hell.

*Proverb 7:1-27*
*1 My son, keep my words, And treasure my commands within you.*
*2 Keep my commands and live, And my law as the apple of your eye.*
*3 Bind them on your fingers; Write them on the tablet of your heart.*
*4 Say to wisdom, "You are my sister," And call understanding your nearest kin,*
*5 That they may keep you from the immoral woman, From the seductress who flatters with her words.*
*6 For at the window of my house I looked through my lattice,*
*7 And saw among the simple, I perceived among the youths, A young man devoid of understanding,*
*8 Passing along the street near her corner; And he took the path to her house*
*9 In the twilight, in the evening, In the black and dark night.*

10 *And there a woman met him, With the attire of a harlot, and a crafty heart.*

11 *She was loud and rebellious, Her feet would not stay at home.*

12 *At times she was outside, at times in the open square, Lurking at every corner.*

13 *So she caught him and kissed him; with an impudent face she said to him:*

14 *"I have peace offerings with me; Today I have paid my vows.*

15 *So I came out to meet you, Diligently to seek your face, And I have found you.*

16 *I have spread my bed with tapestry, Colored coverings of Egyptian linen.*

17 *I have perfumed my bed with myrrh, aloes, and cinnamon.*

18 *Come, let us take our fill of love until morning; Let us delight ourselves with love.*

19 *For my husband is not at home; He has gone on a long journey;*

20 *He has taken a bag of money with him, and will come home on the appointed day."*

21 *With her enticing speech she caused him to yield, with her flattering lips she seduced him.*

22 *Immediately he went after her, as an ox goes to the slaughter, Or as a fool to the correction of the stocks,*

23 *Till an arrow struck his liver. As a bird hastens to the snare, He did not know it would cost his life.*

24 *Now therefore, listen to me, my children; Pay attention to the words of my mouth:*

25 *Do not let your heart turn aside to her ways, Do not stray into her paths;*

26 *For she has cast down many wounded, And all who were slain by her were strong men.*

27 *Her house is the way to hell, Descending to the chambers of death.*

## Prostitutes are referred to as stolen water.

Proverb 9:10-18

10 "The fear of the Lord is the beginning of wisdom, And the knowledge of the Holy One is understanding.

11 For by me your days will be multiplied, And years of life will be added to you.

12 If you are wise, you are wise for yourself, And if you scoff, you will bear it alone."

13 A foolish woman is clamorous; She is simple, and knows nothing.

14 For she sits at the door of her house, On a seat by the highest places of the city,

15 To call to those who pass by, Who go straight on their way:

16 "Whoever is simple, let him turn in here"; And as for him who lacks understanding, she says to him,

17 "Stolen water is sweet, And bread eaten in secret is pleasant."

18 But he does not know that the dead are there, That her guests are in the depths of hell.

## BEWARE OF THE PROSTITUTION BUSINESS

Proverbs 28:20

20 A faithful man will abound with blessings, But he who hastens to be rich will not go unpunished.

Proverbs 28:18

18 Whoever walks blamelessly will be saved, But he who is perverse in his ways will suddenly fall.

Proverbs 10:29

29 The way of the Lord is strength for the upright, But destruction will come to the workers of iniquity.

Romans 1:28-30

28 And even as they did not like to retain God in their knowledge, God gave them over to a debased mind, to do those things which are not fitting;

*29 being filled with all unrighteousness, sexual immorality, wickedness,
covetousness, maliciousness; full of envy, murder, strife, deceit, evil-mindedness; they are whisperers,*
*30 backbiters, haters of God, violent, proud, boasters, **inventors of evil
things**, disobedient to parents. . .*

## BEWARE OF DOWNPLAYING HELL

A big problem in the church of today is that many are doing away with hell. Some in the leadership of the church have
decided to only emphasize the love of God. These unwise leaders have concluded that a loving God would not send people to a
place like hell. Other unwise leaders think that frank discussions
about hell will drive people away from the church. Therefore, in
many churches today, you will never hear about the place called
"hell." But if we view the subject of hell in the way that God
does, we see this important topic as a deterrent to sin. When
people are told the truth about hell, they tend to get serious
about avoiding it.

*2 Peter 2:1-2*
*1 But there were also false prophets among the people, even as there will be false
teachers among you, who will secretly bring in destructive heresies, even denying
the Lord who bought them, and bring on themselves swift destruction.*
*2 And many will follow their destructive ways, because of whom the way
of truth will be blasphemed.*

*2 Timothy 4:3-4*
*3 For the time will come when they will not endure sound doctrine, but
according to their own desires, because they have itching ears, they will heap
up for themselves teachers;*
*4 and they will turn their ears away from the truth, and be turned aside
to fables.*

## BEWARE OF YOUR WORDS

Your words set the position of your will. When your words are against God, your heart grows distant to God.

*Proverbs 18:21*
*21 Death and life are in the power of the tongue, And those who love it will eat its fruit.*

*James 3:3-10*
*3 Indeed, we put bits in horses' mouths that they may obey us, and we turn their whole body.*
*4 Look also at ships: although they are so large and are driven by fierce winds, they are turned by a very small rudder wherever the pilot desires.*
*5 Even so the tongue is a little member and boasts great things. See how great a forest a little fire kindles!*
*6 And the tongue is a fire, a world of iniquity. The tongue is so set among our members that it defiles the whole body, and sets on fire the course of nature; and it is set on fire by hell.*
*7 For every kind of beast and bird, of reptile and creature of the sea, is tamed and has been tamed by mankind.*
*8 But no man can tame the tongue. It is an unruly evil, full of deadly poison.*
*9 With it we bless our God and Father, and with it we curse men, who have been made in the similitude of God.*
*10 Out of the same mouth proceed blessing and cursing. My brethren, these things ought not to be so.*

## BEWARE OF NEGLECTING TO DISCIPLINE YOUR CHILDREN

Disciplining children provides children with protection against sin. Godly parents need to provide firm discipline so that their children will not easily fall into habitual sin patterns.

Note that when the Bible talks about the rod, it is not referring to abuse. Child abuse is a sin.

*Proverb 23:12-14*
*12 Apply your heart to instruction, And your ears to words of knowledge.*
*13 Do not withhold correction from a child, For if you beat him with a rod, he will not die.*
*14 You shall beat him with a rod, And deliver his soul from hell.*

The next verses show us that our heavenly Father disciplines us just as he commands earthly parents to do.

*Hebrews 12:5b-11*
*5 "My son, do not despise the chastening of the Lord, Nor be discouraged when you are rebuked by Him;*
*6 For whom the Lord loves He chastens, And scourges every son whom He receives."*
*7 If you endure chastening, God deals with you as with sons; for what son is there whom a father does not chasten?*
*8 But if you are without chastening, of which all have become partakers, then you are illegitimate and not sons.*
*9 Furthermore, we have had human fathers who corrected us, and we paid them respect. Shall we not much more readily be in subjection to the Father of spirits and live?*
*10 For they indeed for a few days chastened us as seemed best to them, but He for our profit, that we may be partakers of His holiness.*
*11 Now no chastening seems to be joyful for the present, but painful; nevertheless, afterward it yields the peaceable fruit of righteousness to those who have been trained by it.*

## BEWARE OF ABUSING CHILDREN

Abuse of any kind to any one is a sin. There is physical abuse, sexual abuse and emotional abuse. In addition, neglecting a child is a form of abuse. Any abuse against children causes these young ones to begin life with all kinds of hurt and pain. It also puts them in a position to have to deal with difficult unforgiveness issues in their heart.

Children are to be treasured, celebrated, and protected.

*Matthew 18:5-7*
*5 "Whoever receives one little child like this in My name receives Me."*
*6 "But whoever causes one of these little ones who believe in Me to sin, it would be better for him if a millstone were hung around his neck, and he were drowned in the depth of the sea.*
*7 Woe to the world because of offenses! For offenses must come, but woe to that man by whom the offense comes!"*

## BEWARE OF REJECTING WISDOM

*Proverbs 8:11*
*11 For wisdom is better than rubies, And all the things one may desire cannot be compared with her.*

*Proverbs 28:26*
*26 He who trusts in his own heart is a fool, But whoever walks wisely will be delivered.*

## BEWARE OF IGNORING GODLY CORRECTION

*Proverbs 15:10-11*
*10 Harsh discipline is for him who forsakes the way, And he who hates correction will die.*
*11 Hell and Destruction are before the Lord; So how much more the hearts of the sons of men.*

## BEWARE OF COVERING YOUR SINS

*Proverbs 28:13*
*13 He who covers his sins will not prosper, But whoever confesses and forsakes them will have mercy.*

## GOD GIVES SERIOUS ADVICE ABOUT AVOIDING HELL

God gives many strong words about the reality of hell. Here are some of those words for you to review.

*Matthew 18:8-9*
*8 "And if your hand or foot causes you to sin, cut it off and cast it from you. It is better for you to enter into life lame or maimed, rather than having two hands or two feet, to be cast into the everlasting fire.*
*9 And if your eye causes you to sin, pluck it out and cast it from you. It is better for you to enter into life with one eye, rather than having two eyes, to be cast into hell fire."*

*Mark 9:38-48*
*38 Now John answered Him, saying, "Teacher, we saw someone who does not follow us casting out demons in Your name, and we forbade him because he does not follow us."*
*39 But Jesus said, "Do not forbid him, for no one who works a miracle in My name can soon afterward speak evil of Me.*
*40 For he who is not against us is on our side.*
*41 For whoever gives you a cup of water to drink in My name, because you belong to Christ, assuredly, I say to you, he will by no means lose his reward."*
*42 "And whoever causes one of these little ones who believe in Me to stumble, it would be better for him if a millstone were hung around his neck, and he were thrown into the sea.*

*43 And if your hand makes you sin, cut it off. It is better for you to enter into life maimed, than having two hands, to go to hell, into the fire that shall never be quenched –*

*44 where 'their worm does not die and the fire is not quenched.'*

*45 And if your foot causes you to sin, cut it off. It is better for you to enter life lame, rather than having two feet, to be cast into hell, into the fire that shall never be quenched –*

*46 where 'their worm does not die and the fire is not quenched.'*

*47 And if your eye causes you to sin, pluck it out. It is better for you to enter the kingdom of God with one eye, rather than having two eyes, to be cast into hell fire –*

*48 where 'their worm does not die and the fire is not quenched.'"*

APPENDIX

Part One of the Appendix

Part one of the appendix is a verse that I wanted to include because it is a reference to hell, yet it didn't easily fit in any other area of the book.

*Ezekiel 31:15*
*15 "Thus says the Lord God: 'In the day when it went down to hell, I caused mourning. I covered the deep because of it. I restrained its rivers, and the great waters were held back. I caused Lebanon to mourn for it, and all the trees of the field wilted because of it.'"*

Part Two of the Appendix

In the first chapter of the book, it says that the appendix will contain all the verses about outer darkness. These verses are Matthew 8:12, Matthew 22:13, and Matthew 25:30. Those verses are listed here. In addition, they are listed in context, so notice that not only the verses that have the words "outer darkness" are written, but verses that are important to the context of outer darkness are written as well. It is important to include these verses, yet their length could create a feeling of disconnection in the text if written in the body of the book.

**OUTER DARKNESS**

*Matthew 8:12*

12 "But the sons of the kingdom will be cast out into outer darkness. There will be weeping and gnashing of teeth."

*Matthew 22:1-14*

1 And Jesus answered and spoke to them again by parables and said:

2 "The kingdom of heaven is like a certain king who arranged a marriage for his son,

3 and sent out his servants to call those who were invited to the wedding; and they were not willing to come.

4 Again, he sent out other servants, saying, 'Tell those who are invited, "See, I have prepared my dinner; my oxen and fatted cattle are killed, and all things are ready. Come to the wedding."'

5 But they made light of it and went their ways, one to his own farm, another to his business.

6 And the rest seized his servants, treated them spitefully, and killed them.

7 But when the king heard about it, he was furious. And he sent out his armies, destroyed those murderers, and burned up their city.

8 Then he said to his servants, 'The wedding is ready, but those who were invited were not worthy.

9 Therefore go into the highways, and as many as you find, invite to the wedding.'

10 So those servants went out into the highways and gathered together all whom they found, both bad and good. And the wedding hall was filled with guests."

11 "But when the king came in to see the guests, he saw a man there who did not have on a wedding garment.

12 So he said to him, 'Friend, how did you come in here without a wedding garment?' And he was speechless.

13 Then the king said to the servants, 'Bind him hand and foot, take him away, and cast him into outer darkness; there will be weeping and gnashing of teeth'"

*14 "For many are called, but few are chosen."*

*Matthew 25:30-46*

*30 "And cast the unprofitable servant into the outer darkness. There will be weeping and gnashing of teeth."*

*31 "When the Son of Man comes in His glory, and all the holy angels with Him, then He will sit on the throne of His glory,*

*32 All the nations will be gathered before Him, and He will separate them one from another, as a shepherd divides his sheep from the goats.*

*33 And He will set the sheep on His right hand, but the goats on the left.*

*34 Then the King will say to those on His right hand, 'Come, you blessed of My Father, inherit the kingdom prepared for you from the foundation of the world:*

*35 for I was hungry and you gave Me food; I was thirsty and you gave Me drink; I was a stranger and you took Me in;*

*36 I was naked and you clothed Me; I was sick and you visited Me; I was in prison and you came to Me.'"*

*37 "Then the righteous will answer Him, saying, 'Lord, when did we see You hungry and feed You, or thirsty and give You drink?*

*38 When did we see You a stranger and take You in, or naked and clothe You?*

*39 Or when did we see You sick, or in prison, and come to You?'*

*40 And the King will answer and say to them, 'Assuredly, I say to you, inasmuch as you did it to one of the least of these My brethren, you did it to Me.'"*

*41 "Then He will also say to those on the left hand, 'Depart from Me, you cursed, into the everlasting fire prepared for the devil and his angels:*

*42 for I was hungry and you gave Me no food; I was thirsty and you gave Me no drink;*

*43 I was a stranger and you did not take Me in, naked and you did not clothe Me, sick and in prison and you did not visit Me.'"*

*44 "Then they also will answer Him, saying, 'Lord, when did we see You hungry or thirsty or a stranger or naked or sick or in prison, and did not minister to You?'*

*45 Then He will answer them, saying, 'Assuredly, I say to you, inasmuch as you did not do it to one of the least of these, you did not do it to Me.'*

*46 And these will go away into everlasting punishment, but the righteous into eternal life."*

## SALVATION PRAYER

After having read this book if you haven't already given your life to Christ Jesus, then you should know that there are things that you need to do to assure your place in heaven. In order to solidify your place in eternity with God through our Lord and Savior Jesus Christ, these are the steps that you need to take:

*Romans 10:9*
*9 If you confess with your mouth the Lord Jesus and believe in your heart that God has raised Him from the dead, you will be saved.*

- Admit that you are a sinner.
- Repent of your sins.
- Believe on the Lord Jesus Christ.
- Accept Jesus as your Lord and Savior by saying a prayer of salvation.

Salvation Prayer:

Heavenly Father,

Here I stand before you admitting that I am a sinner. I ask you to forgive me. I believe that Jesus Christ was crucified on the cross and that He died for my sins. I am ready to turn from my sinful ways. Lord, please come into my heart and life as my personal Savior. Amen

At the conclusion of the prayer of salvation, you are now a part of God's family. You have become a new creature and old things have passed away. Now in order to maintain a strong relationship with your Lord and Savior, you need to:

- Pray and talk to God every day. (1 Thessalonians 5:17)
- Read your Bible. (2 Timothy 2:15)
- Be baptized, fellowship, and serve with other Christians in a church that teaches the gospel of Christ. (Acts 8:26-40, Hebrews 10:25, 1 Corinthians 6:16)
- Tell others about Jesus Christ. (John 4:28-30)

If you have never asked Jesus to forgive you of your sins, then it is important that you do that now. Without forgiveness of your sins by Jesus, you will spend eternity in hell. You must repent of your sins. When you ask Jesus to forgive you of your sins and you invite Him to be Lord of your life, you receive the gift of eternal life in heaven.

## FORGIVENESS OF SINS PRAYER

If you have been reading this book and the Holy Spirit has convicted you of a sin or of sins, you can receive forgiveness and have a new start. Take this opportunity to stop and get things right between you and your heavenly Father.

Dear Lord,

I have a confession to make. I have been reading this book, and I now realize that I have been doing things that you consider sin. I repent of my sins and ask you to forgive me. I want to obey you and follow your commands every day of my life.

Thank you for showing me the truth, and thank you for helping me to obey your will. Amen

*Ephesians 4:30-32*
*30 And do not grieve the Holy Spirit of God, by whom you were sealed for the day of redemption.*
*31 Let all bitterness, wrath, anger, clamor, and evil speaking be put away from you, with all malice.*
*32 And be kind to one another, tenderhearted, forgiving one another, even as God in Christ forgave you.*

## SPECIAL NEEDS PRAYER

If you have problems such as recurring bad thoughts, flash-backs to a time of hurt or trauma such as rape, molestation, pornography involvement, or any sexual involvement with men or women, the following is what you need to pray:

Dear Father,

I ask You in the name of Jesus Christ to set me free from the past. (Name the thing or things that you want to be freed from.) I repent of my role in them. I ask You to forgive me of my sins in these matters. I ask You, Lord, to open my spiritual eyes and ears that I might see and hear Your glory. Open the file cabinet of my heart, soul, mind, and flesh. Father, remove all the files of hurts, traumas, pictures, and people and allow my eyes to see them ascending, upward that I may know that you have removed them, and I thank You, Lord, for setting me free from the past.

Now, Lord, I ask You to fill these files with Your Word and the gifts of the spirit and fruit of the spirit. I ask You to have the angels to close the cabinets and seal them with the blood of Jesus. Amen.

## ABOUT THE AUTHOR

Franklin D. Battle, Sr., has walked in the calling of prophet since the mid-seventies. He studies the word of God with a deep devotion to know as much as humanly possible about God and His kingdom. He has an undaunted zeal and a heart of service to God. He has a God-given desire to spread the gospel throughout the world.

Prophet Battle ministers across America and the continent of Africa speaking the profound word of God in spirit and truth. He takes his calling seriously and delivers the message of God with the love and anointing of God. Many who have heard Prophet Battle minister the Word of God have witnessed countless numbers of miracles, prophecies, and great deliverances. He testifies of having seen Jesus, Satan, angels, and demonic forces, including many visits to the third heaven where he received revelations of our God-given power and also revelations of the networking of Satan's kingdom.

From 1996 to 1999, Franklin Battle planted and served as the Senior Pastor of a church in Miami, Florida, which the Lord instructed him to name Church of the Rock. In 1996, he planted the Upper Room Church in Riverdale, Georgia, where he presently serves as the Senior Pastor.

Prophet Battle is a family man. He has been married to his wife, Prophetess Madelyn Battle, for more than 30 years and has three adult children and three grandchildren. He has worked in many arenas during his lifetime but his lifelong passion is giving glory to God in everything he does. Prophet Battle is very insightful. This makes his books a must read and a great addition to your spiritual library.

To schedule Prophet Battle as a conference speaker, call or write his office:

6538 Church Street
Riverdale, Georgia 30274
(770) 907-7468 phone
(770) 909-3442 fax
fdb@projectreallife.org

IMPORTANT CAUTION:

**Do not bother the high ranks of Satan's kingdom in the heavenly places unless instructed by the Lord. Read on for more information.**

## MY TESTIMONY

## BINDING AND LOOSING

A few years ago the Lord gave me a dream. In that dream, a man was teaching me how to skin rabbits without using a knife. I became very good with this technique. Later I climbed up in a large tree and saw a huge black panther asleep on a limb. I thought to myself, "I will try this new technique on him." So I grabbed the panther by his skin. He moved one of his whiskers and almost knocked me out of the tree. I quickly turned him loose and started to quickly climb further into the tree. Then I woke up, still running from the panther.

## INTERPRETATION OF THE DREAM

The Lord told me that is exactly how principalities react when we bind and attack them. They will come and attack us as well. We are to leave them alone unless God tells us to attack them, because whenever we attack them, we may forget but they never forget. They will look for an opportunity to attack those who attack them. That is why it seems to some people as if they are always under attack.

## BACKGROUND

I had been incorrectly taught that we were to attack the principalities and powers in the heavenly places; therefore, I did this on a regular basis, just to pull them down and have the angels to attack them. On occasion I have had the angels to pull them out of the heavenlies over Russia and other parts of the world for no apparent reason. I thought this was what we were supposed to do. Needless to say, now I do not attack the principalities, powers rulers of darkness, nor the spiritual hosts of wickedness in the heavenly places without orders from the Father. However, this does not mean we can't fight and cast out the demons that are in people. We must do this to set the captives free in the name of Jesus. We are commanded to do this in the Bible.

## WARNING

WARNING!!! DO NOT bother the high ranks of Satan's kingdom in the heaF(venly places unless instructed by the Lord. Rarely are you randomly attacked or provoked by them. If you are, the Lord will allow you to fight back. You are always to remember that they are not usually concerned with us as individuals. They tend to be more involved with national and international things such as wars and global conflicts as well as those believers who demonstrate the type of supernatural powers Jesus demonstrated.